W9-AUO-109

101 Questions Women Ask About Relationships

by
George G. Bloomer

PUBLISHING

All rights reserved. No part of this book may be reproduced in whole or in part without written permission from the publisher, except by a reviewer who may quote brief passages in a review; nor may any part of this book be reproduced, stored in a retrieval system, or transmitted in any form or by any means electronic, mechanical, including photocopying, recording, or other, without permission in writing from the author, except as provided by USA copyright law.

All Scripture quotations are from the King James Version. Used by permission

101 Questions women Ask About Relationships

Copyright © 1999
George G. Bloomer
All rights reserved

Printed in the United States of America

ISBN 1-56229-420-2

Published by PneumaLife Publishing

Dedication

This book is lovingly dedicated to two incredible young women in my life: my awesome daughter, Jessica, and her amazing sister, Jennifer. It was with both of your futures in mind that this project was undertaken. My hope and prayer is that it will prove a beneficial and timely guide to your own relationship experiences, beginning just a few years from now. (And no sooner. I mean it.)

This work is also dedicated to the youth ministry of Beth'el Family Worship Center, Saved, Single and Satisfied. As the committed watcher of your souls, my love extends to see that your natural relationships are properly guided, as well. May God forever keep you in the states your name suggests He's placed you. Except for, perhaps, that condition in the middle.

Credits

Many and much thanks are in order for the completion of this project. I thank God, first, for the dedication and support of every individual who was actively involved. To my wife, Jeanie Bloomer— Thanks for being a visible blessing to and in my fife, and for your early assistance with this book. To Kimberly Meadows and Melanie Holmes—your assistance is greatly appreciated.

Acknowledgments

Many and much thanks are in order for the completion of this literary project. I thank God, first, for the dedication and support of every individual who was actively involved.

To my significant other, Jeanie Bloomer—Thanks for being a visible blessing to and in my life, and for your early assistance with this book.

To my editor, Melanie Holmes—Thanks for unscrambling the words of my mouth, and unraveling the meditations of my heart, and making them acceptable for the printed page.

And to Kimberly Meadows, editing assistant and chief transcriber—Thanks for all of the typing—really.

Introduction

Let me begin by first saying that I am not a relationship guru. I am not a love doctor. Nor a psychologist. Neither am I a sex therapist. In a nutshell, I'm no expert.

This book is born, then, not out of any pretense that I might have of qualification or professional proficiency in the area of male and female relations, but rather out of a desire to help meet a broad-based need within the intimate realms of Christian peoples' lives. My hope is that couples will sit down and read it together, and that single individuals will consider its advice, as well.

Indeed, there is an urgent, dire necessity among Christians in relationship to establish and abide in marital and acceptable pre-marital unions that are healthy, successful, and blessed. I know, because there was a time when I was unsaved, unskilled, and unprosperously involved in relationships myself. Even after receiving salvation, in fact, there were times of questioning in my life when I desperately needed answers and lessons in marriage that I seriously needed to learn. And I did learn—sometimes the hard way.

I am aware, too, that my personal experience is not totally unique, but that there are many romantically involved persons who are in the dark or in the wrong. Over the years, I've quietly but keenly observed the relationships of friends and family members, as well as those of the many confused couples and searching singles who've visited my office for counseling sessions. As a minister, I've had the privilege of holding post as both spiritual and natural advisor, and have heard the stories and situations of married, soon-to-be married, ought-to-get married, won't-ever marry, planning-to-unmarry, and shouldn't-even-be-thinking-about-marrying individuals. The 101 questions contained within this book are, quite simply, theirs. But even after the carefully thought-out responses that I've offered as possible solutions to described romantic problems, I don't profess to know all of the answers.

My sincere desire and prayer is that this publication be used as a tool, not as law or secondary Scripture. It is a tool that we, the Body of Christ, can actually use, nevertheless. The fact of the matter is that fifty-one percent of church marriages end in divorce. While this figure is high, it appears that our tolerance levels are at an all-time low, and no one wants to stick to their choices, or live with the decisions they've made. Two-timing and forbidden relationships are rampant and growing increasingly acceptable, even though the Apostle Paul plainly admonishes us to let every man have his own wife. And subsequently, every woman is to have her own husband.

Speaking of women, females are frequently bearing the greater weight of relationship stress. Statistics tell us that the average man is married between the ages of twenty and twenty-seven, which means that if a woman doesn't find a mate while she is between the ages of nineteen and twenty-six, chances are, she'll be forced to settle down with someone who's already been married. What's more, Satan is ardently deceiving and seducing believers into compromising their Christian values by embracing the demonic ideologies of the world.

Saved folk are consulting psychic hotlines for ungodly advice and seeking astrologers, motivational speakers, self-help institutions, and soap operas for marital and relationship insight. This is due to a lack of knowledge and the absence of faith on the part of some wavering Christians. At the same time, there is a frustrating lack of proper, timely ministerial counseling, which is also to blame. Widely unavailable is church-based guidance and advisement that actually deals with the very human, very realistic situations that surface in and influence the lives of God's people. My prayer is that this book, on the other hand, will be a down-to-earth, reality-based source of natural counseling that will further enhance your spiritual walk, as well.

Again, I reiterate: I'm no expert. God, on the other hand, is, and His Word is a blue-printed guide to righteous living for all aspects of our lives, including the romantic one. Though some may beg to differ, I hold that the Bible does not contain all of the answers to our relationship questions, and we shouldn't expect it to. Romance, passion, and relationships are carnal entities, while the Word is spiritually coded; it was intended by God to be this way. This is certainly not to deny that on multiple levels and in many instances, the Bible does offer us direct and straightforward solutions to our earthly, human problems. Indeed, its ancient characters did experience real, tangible existences, from which we current-day dwellers should take wise and literal example.

But more often than not, I suggest, the Bible provides us with clues. Clues that we need natural and spiritual interpretation in deciphering and aptly applying to our lives. Clues that are meant to whet our appetites, make us spiritually hungry, and send us scrambling for a filling....

Think of me, the author of this text, then, as an experienced but ever-learning chef, if you will, serving you the Word of God, Scriptural insight, and prayerful opinion on the platters of Christian morality, righteous living, and personal experience. There's plenty of satisfying meat, some marrow-filled bones, and even a couple of juicy T-Bone steaks to be had, from the menu of advice that in this lovingly prepared publication. Help yourself to it's time-tested recipes for relationship success.

George G. Bloomer
April 1999

1

Q. How much of an age difference should there be between potential couples, and is it okay for the female to be older than the male?

A. Genesis 17:17
...Shall a child be born to him that is an hundred years old? and shall Sarah, that is ninety years old, bear?

THOUGHT

I see no reason why a younger man and older woman shouldn't marry, but Scripture does indicate that typically men were several years older than their wives. Such was the case for Abraham and Sarah, for example, who were ten years apart. This is not to say that there is necessarily any current-day significance to this fact, but in answer to this question, I feel it necessary to point out the truth about how our biblical forefathers structured their relationships.

Women tend to mature a bit faster than do men, and my experience teaches me that it can be very good and wise for a young lady to date a man a few years older than herself for the sake of intellectual balance. If the younger woman can handle the age difference, then, I believe such a relationship can work. I do have a problem, however, with men who try to talk to girls twenty or so years younger than themselves. It has been my observation that in many marriages where such a great age difference exists—where the husband is twenty or more years older than his wife—the female, sadly, has been robbed of her youth and vitality. But clearly, the decision is the couple's.

2

Q. I'm having problems getting my unsaved husband to respect my designated times of fasting unto the Lord. What should I do?

A. 1 Corinthians 7:5

Defraud ye not one the other, except it be with consent for a time, that ye may give yourselves to fasting and prayer; and come together again, that Satan tempt you not for your incontinency.

THOUGHT

Ask for the wisdom and divine intervention of God, so that the times that you plan to fast and give yourself to the Lord will be the very times when he is tired! God still performs miracles, and He's always in the prayer-answering business. Without question, He will make a way for you to draw nigh unto Him.

3

Q. While it may be true that opposites attract, do opposites really make good marriage partners, or are more similar personalities better suited for a long-lasting relationship?

THOUGHT

Compatibility is an essential component of successful relationships, and "opposites," I have found, can be as equally compatible to each other as are two similar people. Mr. or Mrs. Right, then, could very well be someone quite different from yourself. At the same time, however, there do exist unhappy, unstable marriages, where the partners are incompatible but have very much in common! So compatibility and commonalities are clearly second to...

Commitment. More important than having like personalities, interests, goals, and backgrounds, or being total opposites, it is absolutely essential for current and potential marriage partners to have a true commitment to each other. Eventually, there will come a time in the marriage relationship when the attraction grows old and the passion subsides. This means that were it not for the committed attitudes of some dedicated spouses who choose to uphold their vows, even when the going gets tough, marriages would never last long enough for the bad times to turn into good.

4

Q. How does a single woman with young daughters in the home go about allowing a new man into her life?

THOUGHT

Very prayerfully. This is a very serious question, because if the situation it presents is not handled correctly, the results can be tragic.

I believe that at a certain time in your lives, single mothers, you need to live for your children. Young girls are very tender and often extremely vulnerable, and men are sometimes overly fascinated with youth. Therefore, I think it unwise for you to bring your daughters under the potential romantic threat of a man who's supposed to be your suitor!

It is imperative that you go about your dating situation with extreme care and caution, and that you ask God for patience. If possible, I strongly suggest that you deny yourself any romantic involvement, until the time comes when your daughters have reached an age of independence (which is about the time that they would go off to college) from you and your household. This will better ensure that the man who comes into their mother's life will be able to focus on their mother—you—and not be tempted to molest or seduce them. And if the new man were to make such an attempt, the mature, aware young ladies that you have raised would more than likely be able to ward off their offender, defending themselves until they informed you.

5

Q. Are interracial marriages sanctioned by God, and can marriages between members of different races be as successful as those between members of the same race?

A. Numbers 12:1
And Miriam and Aaron spake against Moses because of the Ethiopian woman whom he had married: for he had married: for he had married an Ethiopian woman.

THOUGHT

Absolutely. According to Scripture, Moses, a Hebrew, married a black woman, and there is no record of him having problems with that relationship, except where a closed-minded family was involved. My experience teaches me that just as Moses and his wife got along, and King Solomon and the Queen of Sheba, who were of different racial backgrounds, loved each other, interracial relationships can be highly successful and blessed.

The question is, will society allow them to be? Going back to the story of Moses and his wife, it was Miriam and Aaron, the people looking on the relationship from the outside, who experienced problems with it. Because they spoke critically of Moses, God dealt with them harshly. Still, all over the world, unions between persons of different races are becoming increasingly popular, successful, and acceptable, and this pleases God. It is what He intended.

Note: While there are Scriptures in the Bible that appear to suggest that only like races should be together, the "races" these Scriptures refer to have nothing to do with skin color or ethnicity. So don't accept the racist teaching that says that God is against interracial unions!

6

Q. Should men as well as women remain virgins until they
are married?

A. 1 Corinthians 7:1-2
... It is good for a man not to touch a woman. Nevertheless,
to avoid fornication, let every man have his own wife, and let
every woman have her own husband.

THOUGHT
   Absolutely. It's the will—and Word—of God.

7

Q. Should a man allow himself to trust and consider for marriage a woman with a "reputation"?

A. Hosea 1:2
...And the Lord said to Hosea, Go, take unto thee a wife of whoredoms and children of whoredoms...

THOUGHT

This is without question a personal call. God had the prophet Hosea marry a known harlot, Gomer, and when she later cheated on Hosea, he willingly took her back. While the story of Hosea and Gomer's relationship is commonly considered a symbolic one, illustrating the adulterous relationship between the unfaithful nation of Israel and God, there was an actual, literal case of marital infidelity between the prophet and his wife. But again, the two of them were able to abide together.

Sometimes a woman of unfavorable reputation needs a man with a decent background to come into her life and apply his good name to her bad one, thus legitimizing her. Sometimes, too, a man can lose out on what would have been an excellent companion for himself because he won't marry a woman with a past; a past that might have been established in unguided youth or ignorance.

But everybody makes mistakes and needs a second chance. If you're a believer, seek God's confirmation and approval for any individual you want to consider for a serious relationship. He'll let you know whether that person is worth your time and effort.

8

Q. Is it true, in a sense, that "all men are dogs"?

THOUGHT

Yes. And we must also understand that women are, too! There is indeed a sexual quality to all of us that is animalistic. It is a part of our human nature, incidentally, and if it is not tamed and brought under subjection through the power of spirituality and discipline, it can lead the most pious of us into perverted activity previously unimagined. Most people aren't aware of the second half to the popular proverbial saying, "Curiosity killed the cat." The moral lies in the conclusion of the story: "But satisfaction brought him back," meaning that unmanned curiosity and perverted interest can lead one into the very activities and behavior they previously considered taboo. As a result, they find that they can no longer live with themselves, and they die or are "killed" of shame and embarrassment. But because people tend to find a lewd "satisfaction" in doing that which is forbidden, they can be "brought back" to life once involved. Excusing their behavior to themselves, they alter their convictions and beliefs and are actually able to live with themselves in the new sinful state.

We should all give the "dog" in each of us the "Bone" of this moral lesson and be mindful not to become our very nemesis, the tampering "cat"!

9

Q. Is the purpose of marriage defeated if a couple decides not to have children, and they marry exclusively for sexual fulfillment?

A. 1 Corinthians 7:1-2

It is good for a man not to touch a woman. Nevertheless, to avoid fornication, let every man have his own wife, and let every woman have her own husband.

THOUGHT

No, it is not wrong to get married for the purpose of having sexual fulfillment, or to avoid having sexual relations outside of marriage, but it probably is wrong to marry an individual just because you feel a sexual attraction toward them.

God recognized a problem in Adam's being all alone in the Garden (He saw that it was "not good"), so He created a "help meet" for him. Adam's sexuality and need for companionship were not ignored by God. He saw their importance, and marriage is an institution designed to satisfy sexual need. But at the same time, the woman God provided Adam was tailor-made for him, as she came from him, being literally fashioned from one of his ribs. Eve was a woman "meet" for Adam, we can assume, in all areas—not just the romantic or intimate one. So when choosing life partners, it is important that we look for more and higher commonalities than mutual passion. A marriage that is to last will have to be based upon more than just sex.

I also believe that if a couple doesn't like or love children, and if they aren't inclined to deal with and rear them properly, they absolutely shouldn't have them. Children are a blessing from God to be offered up to Him. When God sees them incorrectly loved or treated, the faulty parents become accursed in His eyes. So don't enter the realm of parenthood if you aren't qualified.

Also, know that marriage and family are two separate entities: the latter is the combination of parents and children, and the former involves the committed couple exclusively. Regardless of whether or not you bring little ones into the picture, then, always acknowledge the independence of your marriage union from all other associations.

10

Q. Is divorce ungodly?

A. 1 Corinthians 7:10-11
And unto the married I command, yet not I, but the Lord, Let not the wife depart from her husband: But and if she depart, let her remain unmarried, or be reconciled to her husband: and let not the husband put away his wife.

THOUGHT

Yes. God never intended for divorce to become a part of our vocabularies, let alone, a common, dividing factor in the majority of our marriage experiences. I believe divorce breaks the heart of God. He intended for couples to stay together — the Scripture tells us so. Know that when God first instituted marriage, divorce was not a part of His plan. Because of the hardness of men's hearts, nevertheless, He has permitted it.

I certainly do believe that there are cases where married couples need to divorce, and after looking at many different circumstances and situations, I now freely advise certain couples to go ahead with their intended separation, remarry if they want to, get on with their lives, and just enjoy the time the have left on earth. The truth of the matter is that some individuals were never meant to be married in the first place, as many of them haven't learned how to abide peaceably as singles. Even so, they'll get married and wreak havoc in the life of another individual, never learning the lessons of successful marriage before they go off and tie the knot with someone else!

11

Q. My partner refuses to confront me with the problem areas in our marriage. How do I proceed?

THOUGHT

My advice to you is to leave it alone and pray. Timing is everything in a marriage relationship, especially when a couple has spent years together, because by then, the two of them know each other. They know the times of when and when not to approach each other in certain areas, or with certain concerns.

If you are not at a place in your relationship where you really know your mate, only time, again, will bring this closeness about. Seek God, then, for time's gift, which is the insight into who your spouse really is, and the ways in which you can and cannot approach them, as well as the knowledge of the proper time to address specific issues—such as the present difficulties in your marriage—with them.

12

Q. My husband calls me a nagger and says that all I do is whine and complain. The way I see it, EVERYTHING I say and do is somehow annoying to him! Is the problem really with me, or is it with him?

THOUGHT

My impression is that it's with BOTH of you! I don't mean to sound irritated or cross, but really—the two of you need to stop the nonsense and grow up!

You are both adults, aren't you? You did vow to love and honor each other, right? Then commit yourselves to finding out what ticks the other off—your nagging annoys him, his indifference bothers you—and Stop Doing It!

13

Q. Does God view virgins differently than He does non-virgins?

A. 1 Corinthians 7:37
Nevertheless he that standeth steadfast in his heart, having no necessity, but hath power over his own will, and hath so decreed in his heart that he will keep his virgin, doeth well.

THOUGHT

Certainly He does. Men and women who retain their virginity are undefiled by the opposite sex, and because they are untouched, they are inherently virtuous. The fact of the matter is that anytime you forego sexual intercourse and involvement, you hear more and better from God. And the more in tune you are with the Almighty, the more pleased He becomes with you. Those of us who are married to Christ and a natural spouse, who at allotted times commit ourselves to proper fasting from sexual intimacy, know this to be very much true.

14

Q. Is there such a thing as perversion in the marriage bed?

A. Hebrews 13:4
Marriage is honorable in all, and the bed undefiled: but whoremongers and adulterers God will judge.

THOUGHT

Yes. I say that the most serious and common way in which the bed of a married couple is defiled, or perverted, is not in what the couple does together in that bed, but by what happens when one of the marriage partners commits mental adultery. Allow me to clarify.

Under ancient Hebrew law, if a man committed the act of adultery, he was punished by death. But Jesus, who came to fulfill the law, saw the issue of adultery as beginning long before the illegal intimacy even took place. In Matthew 5:22-28, He said, "Ye have heard that it was said by them of old time, Thou shalt not commit adultery: But I say unto you, That whosoever looketh on a woman to lust after her hath committed adultery with her already in his heart." Clearly, this Scripture speaks to the married man, for only a man with a wife can commit the "adultery" that the Word speaks of. [The Scripture doesn't speak of "fornication", mind you, which is sexual relations between unmarried individuals.] This means that while a single man can look at various women freely and without consequence, if a married man looks on another woman with lust, although he may never physically touch her, he has committed the sin of adultery. Then, if he goes home to be with his wife, he does further damage because he defiles their bed!

Because mental adultery is so prevalent, it is not uncommon for the spirit of a third party (a past lover, object of desire, or love interest of one of the married partners) to possess a typical marriage bedroom, either often, or from time to time, through the explicit imagination or memory of one of the spouses. It must be said that this practice is nothing less than the outgrowth of Perversion, who is an unclean spirit. Whether illicit thoughts for another are admitted to by the offending spouse, or not, it is extremely disrespectful to the partner being downplayed by the memory of the outsider and is most displeasing to God. For Christian men and women who don't want this type of sin on their hands and in their hearts, discipline — of the flesh, and regarding the vow of commitment to one specific partner, and that partner only — must be achieved on a daily basis. It is a walk of faith and faithfulness.

15

Q. I happen to be aware of another married Christian's infidelity. What are my responsibilities? In other words, should I tell their spouse or pastor?

A. Proverbs 25:9
Debate thy cause with thy neighbor himself; and discover not a secret to another.

THOUGHT
   I say NO, not even if you are the one with whom they were unfaithful (You didn't think I knew, did you?).
   Seriously, though, all I can tell you is mind your business and pray for them. You may very well be aware that there was cheating, but what you aren't aware of are the ins and outs of that person's relationship with their spouse. There's no telling what undue, irreparable damage your wagging tongue might cause. Allow that individual to confess his or her own faults to God, their spouse, or their pastor if they so choose. In the end they must account for their deed, and it's their soul that has to answer to God.

16

Q. There are some things in my pre- and post-marital past that I fear would hurt the relationship between my spouse and me if I were to confess them. Am I allowed to keep these things to myself, without being guilty of dishonesty?

THOUGHT

While confession is good for the soul, it is not always good for everybody else around us. Unwisely, many spiritual leaders and self-improvement gurus are heavily into the business of advising that things of the past be suddenly revealed in the present. Unfortunately, this is wreaking unnecessary havoc in relationships that were going fine! This is not to say that couples shouldn't be honest and up-front with each other. Indeed, there are issues and incidents that we must share with each other (sometimes our spouse's health or life will actually depend on our truth-telling, if you know what I mean...), but we have to be able to distinguish between what past and present occurrences need to be disclosed, and what we really ought to keep to ourselves.

My advice is that you know your spouse thoroughly, which includes knowing what information they can and cannot handle. This knowledge is beneficial to you, your mate, and the health of your relationship. Even if we are individuals in relationship, some things in our lives were meant to be ours alone. "Selective confession," then, is part of our right to privacy as individuals. It has nothing to do with being dishonest, and everything to with being wise.

17

Q. How do I uphold an order I have received from the Lord that my unbelieving spouse opposes?

A. 1 Corinthians 7:14
For the unbelieving husband is sanctified by the wife, and the unbelieving wife is sanctified by the husband...

THOUGHT

Prayerfully. For this, you need to consult God for the speedy conversion or compliance of your spouse because of the obstacle they pose to your spiritual walk and obedience to God. Trust God and have faith that change will soon come and continue to live a sanctified life before your mate. This is all that you can do, until the Lord intervenes and moves them out of your way, out of your life, or into His fold.

18

Q. The only reason my partner and I are still together is because of our children. Is this really our obligation?

THOUGHT

This depends on whether or not your situation is tolerable. If there was a problem of emotional or physical abuse between you and your partner, or any equally extreme situation or circumstance dividing the two of you, my advice would be to separate. It would be better for both you and the children. On the other hand, if minor disagreements, petty disputes, and even some bigger conflicts were making you less than amiable toward each other, and you did have young children, I'd probably say, "Yes, you are obligated to stick it out for as long as possible for the sake of the little ones." So pray and trust God for the proper solution to your particular situation.

19

Q. Between Christian couples, how long should dating last before marriage? Is there a time after which an engagement is too long?

THOUGHT

This topic is more thoroughly addressed in Question 95, but I sense that the attitude of your inquiry is a little different from that of the person to come, so I will give you my opinion.

I think that the couple themselves must determine how long their courtship or engagements should last. I believe they should make sure that it doesn't last too short or too long. But find a balanced time frame.

The longer you remain close friends with a person, the more you get to know them. Who they are, what makes them tick, and what is unfavorable about them. Not only do you begin to see what you like in them, you also start to realize what you don't like. Of course, when you're dating a person, especially with the intent to marry, you really should get to know how much, or how little, you like that individual. The truth about people in relationship is that the longer they stay together, the more likely they are to start nit-picking at each other. If you're finding out what really turns you off about an individual before you've actually turned on the commitment and married that person (which means, presumably, that you couldn't just pick up and leave, when things got rough), you're not being fair to them, and you're doing yourself a disservice. Marriage is a discovery, a journey, an act of faith, and a commitment. If you hold things off for too long and start criticizing before you commit, it's very likely you won't ever settle on or settle down with that person. A person who just might've been the very best choice for you.

20

Q. Is it okay for Christians to elope?

THOUGHT

Yes, if that is what they wish to do. Other ministers will disagree with me here, as they valuable the more traditional church ceremony, but I recognize that there are individuals out there for whom eloping is more convenient. Two people's desire to marry in virtual secrecy could be for the sake of expedience, privacy, whim, or the need to uninvolve opposing family members. Whatever the reasons, nevertheless, I say it's the couple's right and decision to make.

Q. My wife and I have a nontraditional arrangement, where I stay home and care for the kids and household, while she goes outside to work. Is there anything wrong with our system?

THOUGHT

Not as far as I can tell, sir. Role reversal in modern-day society is discussed in Question 100, but the point is that what you and your wife do for the proper function and smooth operation of your household is your business. The Bible says nothing against the husband and father being the nurturer/ caretaker, nor against the wife and mother being the primary breadwinner. It sounds as if the arrangement has you and your wife's mutual agreement and consent, so carry on. A man's gotta do what a man's gotta do. And so does his woman.

22

Q. How many times is too many for remarriage?

THOUGHT

To people who find themselves marrying time and time again, I must say that you evidently are not dealing with reality. Neither are you learning anything from each of your consecutive relationships!

I have found that in most cases where a man has been married three and four times, or more, from wife number three and upward, there was usually a very quick courtship (something like four or five months of dating). This often happens because the man is under pressure from the woman to commit, or because he is so used to living with and being taken care of by a lady, he refuses to slow down, wait, and really get to know his fiancée properly before tying the knot. So his personal needs and weaknesses cause him act too soon. This is often the problem with women who find themselves marrying more than twice, as well.

Men and women who remarry that many times are victims of the "Changing Socks" syndrome. There's a problematic "hole" in all of their relationships with the opposite sex. Instead of recognizing it as something serious that needs to be addressed and dealing with it, they choose to throw away the current "mate." They think the offense lies in someone other than themselves and quickly set out to select a new one. But, brethren, these things ought not be.

Here is a bit of advice, some expressly delivered wisdom of George: It is impossible to do something the same way over and over again and get different results. Period. For the wise, I trust that this will be sufficient.

23

Q. Some people say that married people and single folks shouldn't "hang out" together. A married woman shouldn't have as her best friend a single woman, because the single woman's lifestyle of freedom will distract the married woman from her marital duties. Is this unreasonable?

THOUGHT

No, I wouldn't say that it is. In many cases, a single woman will unwittingly flaunt her freedom before her married girlfriend to the point where the married woman begins to feel she is losing out on life. The sad thing is that in many instances, the married woman is losing out, because she's gotten married too soon, is married to the wrong person, or her husband is not very pleasant to live with. Of course, the same can be true for a married man who has a bunch of bachelor buddies. The main thing is to stick with the choice you've made, whether it be to be married or single, and adhere to the commitment therewith. If you are a single person, don't point out to your married friends how wonderful your independent lifestyle is, compared to the burdens of marriage. By the same token, if you are already married, it's probably okay to try to encourage your unattached friends to find a life partner, especially if they can see that your marriage is a happy, successful one. Don't gripe to them about how you wish you had never married that so-and-so-and-so-and-so. If you're in a marriage relationship and change is indeed what you want, and you have legitimate cause to desire it, seek the all-wise counsel of God, not the uninformed advice of your swinging-single associates.

24

Q. Does the Bible explicitly say that sexual relations are to exist exclusively within the bonds of marriage, or is this merely a law of tradition instituted by man for the sake of order and custom?

A. 1 Thessalonians 4:3-5
For this is the will of God, even your sanctification, that ye should abstain from fornication: That every one of you should know how to possess his vessel in sanctification and honor; Not in the lust of concupiscence, even as the Gentiles which know not God...

THOUGHT

If abstaining from premarital intimacy is a tradition and custom of man's design, it's been blatantly overlooked and ignored since inception and probably first went unheeded by the very man who invented it!

Actually, it is God's will and intention that no man have sexual relations with a woman unless he is married to her, and vice-versa. The Word of God is very explicit on this issue. To show you God's clear will on this issue, I've compiled a special list of Scriptures, the bulk of which are found in 1 Corinthians that explicitly address the topic of fornication (sexual relations outside of the covenant of marriage). My prayer is that these Scriptures will help further your understanding and increase your faith. Also, see Questions 6 and 13 for discussions on the issue of virginity.

25

Q. My wife frequently discusses the personal issues of our marriage with her girlfriends, even though she knows I don't appreciate this. What can I say to get her to stop publicizing our private business before I lose my temper?

A. Ephesians 4:26
Be ye angry and sin not: let not the sun go down upon your wrath...

THOUGHT

It's understandable that this situation is making you furious, but you must continue to control yourself until you figure out a way to get through to your wife.

You can begin by reminding yourself that you love your wife, and that she loves you. And if she does indeed love you, and has fully committed herself to you, she must be respectful of your wishes. For your own part, make sure that your spouse is not pouring her heart out to friends because of your unwillingness to discuss issues with her. Let her know that it is your listening ear that is the most important one available to her. Finally, convey to your wife the seriousness of her conversations with outsiders by telling her how it makes you feel: betrayed, unrespected, unsupported, angry. If she's truly committed to you, she will stop this inconsiderate behavior.

(1) *1 Corinthians 5:1-6*
(2) *1 Corinthians 6:9*
(3) *1 Corinthians 6:13*
(4) *1 Corinthians 6:18-20*
(5) *1 Corinthians 7:2*
(6) *1 Corinthians 10:8*
(7) *Hebrews 13:4*

26

Q. In my church, it is taught that a woman should not date a man unless they both plan to marry. What are your views on dating for single women?

THOUGHT

Of course, the Bible says to flee even the appearance of evil. However, in these time in which we live, it is very important to get to know the person you plan to wed and this will often involve fellowship outside of the church. Seeing a person within the confines of the church sometimes give a false sense of security that this is the "ideal" mate. You should, however, use caution not to use dating as a pastime.

As a young Christian woman, you should always carry yourself in a dignified manner and set a standard that demands respect. It is, in my opinion, okay to date someone who you don't plan to marry as long as the other party is clear on this agreement.

27

Q. The Bible speaks of the man as being a "covering" for the woman, but I feel that my husband leaves me exposed, so to speak, by not defending or fully supporting me in times of crisis. Isn't this his duty?

THOUGHT

Not all men are strong enough to give their wives what they need. It sounds to me as if the two of you are unequally yoked in the area of emotional understanding and support. Pray and ask God for a solution and include in that supplication a request for revelatory knowledge concerning the man you have married. When you receive the answer, if you can possibly live with it, you will be blessed for accepting your man for who he is.

28

Q. If you marry someone, only to realize later on that they are not who God intended for you, how do you rectify the situation?

THOUGHT

You don't. Pray and stick to your choice. If you are to be separated from your partner, the Lord will work it out for you, but don't attempt to do the severing. Make sure that you haven't only realized that your mate is "not who God intended for you" because you've recently seen and liked someone new!

Q. Although I'm married and love my husband, I've fallen deeply in love with another man. I want to be delivered from this state, because I know that I can't have both of them, but don't know who to choose, or how to get free. Please tell me how to break the bonds that are connecting my heart to this other man's... if that is indeed what I need to do.

THOUGHT

Ahhhh...this is a tough one. I'm sure you've heard all of the Scriptures concerning adultery, and that you know the wrongness of extra-marital love and affairs, but you're telling me that it's just about too late for "Thou shalt not," because your heart is already involved. You're already feeling strongly, deeply for this other guy.

Obviously, you allowed him to get too close. Now you are in a quagmire of emotional confusion that's causing you to sink. I wish through some strong, spiritual Scripture, I could toss you a rope and pull you out. I truly sense the urgency and seriousness of your situation. But the reality is that only God can supply you an answer on this one, so you must ask Him. Pray about the circumstance, try not to lose your focus, and don't in any way act upon your feelings without first submitting them to the Lord. Know that God is there for you, and that He will help you do the right thing. Because He wants to help you and you want His help, your deliverance is sure to come.

30

Q. I'm pastor of a church where the man and woman of a recently divorced couple are active members. Should they be allowed to date and/or eventually remarry single individuals within the church?

THOUGHT

If your church allows divorce, then technically, they have the right, but in no wise would I encourage them to do this. And I would have to say definitely not, if one or both of the previous partners involved were ministers. As a spiritual leader, they are public examples to both the internal congregation and the outside community.

Here is an extra bit of advice: the number one thing a pastor, preacher, minister, or other high-ranking church official should do when he or she finds the marriage going sour is to make sure that every possible means for reconciliation has been pursued. This is also my advice to divorce-seeking couples who are not church leaders, as well, but it is especially important that God's appointed and anointed individuals act godly. The sad truth, nevertheless, is that in nearly every case of potential break-up that I've counseled, there has been a means by which the couple could remain together, yet they all refused the option.

31

Q. My spouse is unsaved and our relationship is not a good one. Since my mate won't suggest or initiate divorce, am I allowed to do so?

A. 1 Corinthians 7:13-14
And the woman which hath a husband that believeth not, and if he be pleased to dwell with her, let her not leave him. For the unbelieving husband is sanctified by the wife, and the unbelieving wife is sanctified by the husband...

THOUGHT

There is no getting around the Word of God, so the answer to your question, simply, is NO. The soul of your mate is what's most important, and your staying with them could mean the difference between their salvation and eternal damnation. Ask God for deliverance from within, so that you'll have relative peace while you remain there. If He doesn't see fit to bring reconciliation to the relationship between you and your spouse, He'll have them depart, or provide you a way of escape that you won't have had to initiate. Wait on the Lord.

32

Q. What does the Bible say about same-sex marriages and relationships? If some people are born homosexual, how do they reason this with God?

A. Leviticus 18:22; 1 Corinthians 6:9
Thou shalt not lie with mankind, as with womankind: It is an abomination....Know ye not that the unrighteous shall not inherit the kingdom of God? Neither fornicators...nor effeminate, nor abusers of themselves with mankind....

THOUGHT

Homosexuality is a curse placed upon an individual by the spirit of perversion. The perversion spirit can attack a person with this sexual sin at any stage in life, including childhood, or even, I believe, as early as conception. Perversion is a foul, unclean spirit, and all of its offspring—homosexuality included—are offensive to God. In fact, the Word tells us that same-sex relations, and thereby, same-sex marriages, are an abomination to the Lord, meaning that they are sins exceptionally hated or loathed by Him. Therefore, those "Christians" who practice it not only defile and condemn their own spirits, but they greatly displease God.

The way for an affected individual to "reckon" his condition with God is to realize that it is not God who makes homosexuals. God makes men, and it is Satan who perverts them. The duty of a man or woman who is sexually perverted, then, is to acknowledge to God that their desire and practice is indeed wrong, to repent and seek God's deliverance from the perverted spirit, and most importantly, *to stop doing it.*

For those who don't confess Christ, however, homosexuality is not a spiritual issue, but rather a moral question. Traditionally, it is something that society has taught against and even outlawed at one time. Unfortunately, however, this sexual sin and all other types of immoral activity are becoming increasingly acceptable in America today. Undoubtedly, such widespread tolerance, acceptance, and permissiveness will lead this country down a path of moral degradation, and to a demise that will mirror what happened to Sodom and Gomorrah.

33

Q. After months of witnessing to and fellowshipping with an incarcerated man, I have fallen in love with him. Since he has repented of his sins and professes to love me too, I see no reason why I shouldn't commit to him until he is out of prison, after which we'll marry. My church and family are opposed to the whole relationship, however. How, then, should I proceed?

THOUGHT

Very, very carefully. I do not want to underestimate another's faith or salvation, but my experience teaches me that persons who are incarcerated often use religion as a crutch and/or a con. What I have to say to you is this: be wise, beware, be careful, be sure, and be prayerful!

34

Q. For the couple who's dated seriously for quite some time and do intend to marry, how well should they seek to know each other (excluding sexually) before tying the knot? Is there such a thing as being too nosy, or too informed, concerning one's potential mate?

THOUGHT

No, I don't think legitimate concern about a possible mate is wrong. After all, this is the person with whom you intend to spend the entire remaining portion of your life. If ever there were a time to be informed about someone, now is that time! I say for you to jump into that person's history, their present, and what they plan for the future with both feet!

35

Q. What are the rules for single Christians who date? If they are determined not to get involved sexually before marriage, what should be the limits concerning their contact and their conversation with one another?

A. Ephesians 2:3
Among whom also we all had our conversation in times past in the lusts of our flesh, fulfilling the desires of the flesh and of the mind....

THOUGHT

I believe that conversation is the very gateway through which two interested persons enter the realm of physical intimacy. So, usually, before there's any touching, there's a whole lot of talking going on.

For women, the frequent verbal exchange is part of a natural female tendency to communicate. For the man, on the other hand, incessant conversation is usually only his accommodation to the female—it's part of his seduction ritual. For if he obliges her the need to discuss, he can eventually get her to oblige his physical need.

The general rule for dating couples, then, would be to apply discipline. Discipline has to be the governing agent when it comes to sexuality, which natural relationships are essentially all about, because the needs and desires of the flesh are so powerful, they can be overpowering. The very nature of the flesh means that it is always wanting, anyway, and it isn't helped any when the factors of couplehood—attraction, compatibility, curiosity, even love—are added to it before there is an actual marriage commitment. So if couples are disciplined about what and how much they say, they've taken the first crucial step toward disciplining their sexuality.

30

Q. Although I am a confessing Christian, I recently had a baby out of wedlock. How do I deal with the shame of my error, particularly in the face of neighbors, relatives, and members of my church, all of whom seem to be acting as if they are now doubtful of my salvation?

A. Philippians 2:12
...Work out your own salvation with fear and trembling.

THOUGHT

Sometimes a little shame is good. In many cases, it can prevent us from repeating a mistake and help build our character. Since you are a believer, do the right thing and repent. Then love your child and move on.

Don't allow yourself to be shaken by the "Christians" and community who want to condemn you, because salvation is personal, and as long as you've accepted that God has forgiven you, your redemption is sealed. Know, too, that because of ignorance and high-mindedness, many believers fail to display the love and compassion of Christ. In fact, they probably believe it's God who has authorized them to condemn and throw stones at you! None of them are without blemishes of their own!

Through all of this, I believe that you will be made strong if you keep the faith and focus on strengthening your relationship with the Lord. You can also take comfort in the knowledge that through your testimony of perseverance and victory, you will be able to help others who find themselves in a similar circumstance and predicament.

37

Q. Is it against Christian principles, in any shape or form, for me to refuse to change my surname to that of my new husband? What if I choose to include his name as an attachment to my own?

THOUGHT

This issue is a completely personal one. It's something that you need to discuss with your husband; something that the two of you need to work out. And I'll end it here, because there's really no need to drag Christianity, or the Bible—or me, either—into it.

38

Q. I'm in love with a Christian man who is HIV positive. Is it okay if I marry him?

THOUGHT

Because I don't know of any Scriptural passage in the Word of God that speaks against marrying ill or diseased persons, I must say that, biblically speaking, it is all right for the two of you to marry. It is a very serious matter, nevertheless, one that will require your absolute certainty and commitment, should you decide to become this man's spouse. Realize that you will not only have to protect your own health, but for a great part of the relationship, you're going to be your husband's nurse, and not his wife.

39

Q. I am the parent of a teenage boy and girl. At what age should I allow them to begin dating, and is it fair if I make the rules for my daughter a little stricter than those for my son?

THOUGHT

The age at which a young person should begin dating depends solely upon the principles and foundations laid out in his/her home structure. I don't want to begin to sound like a love guru, or sex therapist, by dictating to folks what should happen concerning their love lives, so this one is on you, parent. I do recommend that you look for maturity in your children, however, before allowing them to date, because relationships are only for the mature.

Also, I concur with your insight into the need to monitor your daughter a little more closely than your son. It's really not an issue of "fairness"; it's about protecting the naturally vulnerable, and you should probably explain this to your daughter and son so he'll know to defend his female companions. The violent nature of our society has only made the vulnerability of women that much more evident. Make sure you teach your children safety and common sense.

40

Q. My husband complains about my housekeeping and cooking skills. We cannot discuss it without getting into a big argument. He says that I am not properly fulfilling my wifely duties?

THOUGHT

I must say that I find his attitude toward your relationship rather disturbing. Particularly because in my own household, all of the work is shared: from the cleaning of the house, to the shopping for the groceries, to the transporting of the children back and forth to school. My wife and I share the load of family obligations.

He sounds like a man with old traditional ideas concerning male and female roles, and most of that thinking is probably outdated. One of the two of your ways of thinking is going to have to give...and it shouldn't necessarily be the wife's!

My suggestion is this: if he would like you to cook good meals, have him prepare a decent meal for you! In other words, whatever he is expecting you to do, he must also be willing to do as well. You have no obligation to return the favor, of course, but through a servant attitude he will learn to consider you his equal.

41

Q. I've waited for so long to get married and have now finally met a nice guy. Unfortunately, however, he isn't saved. Should I turn down his marriage proposal until he gives his life to Christ?

A. 2 Corinthians 6:14
Be not unequally yoked together with unbelievers: for what fellowship hath righteousness with unrighteousness? and what communion hath light with darkness?

THOUGHT

Well, you know that I am a traditional Christian. And being that I am a traditional Christian, I have a traditional answer. And that answer is yes. You should wait until your friend is saved, or either find another who is.

The Bible already forewarns us who chose to marry that there will be "trouble in the flesh," even if both partners are believers. But problems are only prolonged and magnified when one spouse is a Christian, and the other is not, possibly even more so than when both partners are unsaved! The simple fact of the matter is that while the two of you probably could love each other, since you wouldn't both love Christ, there would surely be trouble upon trouble in your relationship. So heed the Word and don't walk into a hurricane knowing that already it is one.

42

Q. My wife accuses me of being "unromantic." How do I learn to become a Casanova?

THOUGHT

Quite frankly, your goal shouldn't be to become a Casanova. It should be to become a pleasing husband to your wife. And the only way for you to do this, to become satisfying to her, is to stop trying to figure out what it is that turns her on and simply ask her! Then ask God to help you make the changes.

43

Q. I'm a single woman attending a very strict, orthodox church, where certain recreational activities are prohibited. This is causing problems for me as far as dating is concerned, because there isn't much I can do with the young men I'm interested in, besides invite them to church! What should I do?

A. Galatians 5:1
Stand fast therefore in the liberty wherewith Christ hath made us free, and be not entangled again with the yoke of bondage.

THOUGHT
    Find another church. The one you're in is evidently binding you. Not only are those shackles around your spiritual life not supposed to be there, but they are now actually pinching your physical being, as well, particularly in the area of romance. Break away, right away, from that controlling ministry under which you are being manipulated and go forth in the freedom that God intended for you to have when he first saved you from the bondage of sin. He certainly didn't emancipate you only for you to become enslaved all over again.

44

Q. I have a terrible tendency of always picking the wrong man to get involved with. How can I know ahead of time, before I wind up getting hurt, if a man I like is any good for me?

THOUGHT

In biblical times, young men and women under Hebraic custom did not make their own dating and marriage choices. Rather, their mates were wisely chosen for them by their parents, based upon a number of careful consideration, including lineage, background, and compatibility.

Of course, we are not living in Bible times today, so we have to select our own relationship partners. Still, I am convinced that we need to be as selective in our choice of partners as were the Hebrews. So determine what it is exactly that you want and need in a relationship partner, then set a standard that you don't compromise. In addition, know that timing and patience are everything to the success of a relationship, and that the ideal one for you will happen in due season.

45

Q. My husband and I never communicate like we used to. How do I encourage him to be more vocal and responsive?

A. Proverbs 4:7
. . .And with all thy getting, get understanding.

THOUGHT

While it's probably true that the majority of men are not as vocal and prone to converse as women, the problem could be that the two of you aren't finding any topics of mutual interest to discuss. If you are attempting to discuss with your spouse what really doesn't interest him, you can't reasonably expect any real, genuine communication to go on between the two of you. At the same time, you need to get to know your mate thoroughly. If he happens to be the silent type, you must learn to accept and appreciate this quality in him.

All the same, I encourage you to find out what it is that your mate is passionate about. Know what themes and topics excite and motivate him, and see if you can share his enthusiasm on these subjects. If you learn to "speak his language," the two of you will begin to better understand and relate to each other, and eventually, he may get back to being more verbally responsive to you by discussing your favorite topics and addressing issues you suggest. We can't always expect, however, that the hours-long conversation and exchanges that we shared with our partners when we first began dating them, and were just getting to know them, will have the same frequency and intensity once we become married and have grown somewhat used to and familiar with each other. We shouldn't take our partners for granted, or assume that we've learned all there is to know about them, or allow the romance to grow stale. We must accept the fact that the dynamics of courtship and marriage are quite different from each other.

46

Q. My husband has a tendency of doing things that are supposed to have our mutual understanding and agreement before being undertaken, without first asking my permission. Instead, he chooses to simply "apologize" to me later, by buying me either dinner or a new dress. How do I get him to realize that I'd rather have him show me the honor and respect of asking me beforehand?

THOUGHT

Convey to your husband that he is building what I call a "Camel/Straw" relationship with you by making you endless empty promises and countless void apologies. In other words, there will come a time when you will reach a final "last-straw" incident, where he does what he wants without your permission. At that time, no gift or apology will be able to prevent your "back from breaking," or your patience with him from finally running out. No matter how insignificant that last incident is, the weight or pressure of it will be just too much. Once it's added to all the misdeeds of the past, you'll reach a no-turning-back point and explode on him! He'll get the message and start getting your approval first, if you describe to him what'll happen if he doesn't stop disrespecting you. Be firm and very clear with your husband when you tell your him to quit piling on all the garbage!

47

Q. My husband and I haven't been able to agree on attending the same church, yet the two ministries where we fellowship separately are so different from each other, they cause us to disagree and argue over spiritual issues. Should I simply become a member of his church to bring some peace into our relationship?

A. Matthew 5:9
Blessed are the peacemakers: for they shall be called the children of God.

THOUGHT

Peace is indeed what your relationship needs at this point, so my advice to you is to become a peacemaker. Actually, peace is about having patience when you're under pressure. There is a way for you to possibly relieve yourself of the pressure under which you are currently living, due to the spiritual conflict between you and your spouse: seriously consider attending his place of worship. I know that's difficult to both hear and do, but there's really no other way I can advise you on this one. (And you can be certain that if your husband had first sought my advice on this issue, I would have told him to consider leaving his church for yours.)

48

Q. I'm a former homosexual who is now living a life of deliverance from my past sexual sins. Can I now begin to pursue members of the opposite sex, or should I forever remain single and celibate?

THOUGHT

No, I believe that it is fine for you to begin to pursue members of the opposite sex. I would say for you to only make sure that your deliverance is certain and complete, so that you don't cause a young person to fall in love with you, only for them to find out later on that they could never have a life with you.

49

Q. I recently found out that some time ago, my spouse was un-faithful. Not only am I hurt that the extra-marital affair even oc-curred, but my mate is not even the one who told me it happened, so I am especially wounded by the fact that they were not honest with me. How do I deal with my feelings of anger, betrayal, and lost trust?

THOUGHT

Anger, betrayal, and lost trust... Anger, betrayal, and lost trust. These are such deep, powerful emotions, and the issue surround-ing them is such a sensitive one that the absolute first thing I must recommend before confronting your mate is prayer. Then, after prayer, you'll have to weigh out on your emotional scales on how you want to proceed with the relationship once you've asked your-self and your spouse some crucial questions, such as:

(1) Is this too sensitive an issue to address at this time?

(2) How long ago did the infidelity occur?

(3) How involved was he with the other person? Was it love?

(4) Was this incident really something my mate could have shared with me, and if he had, how would I have handled it?

(5) What were the reasons for his not telling me—his protection or mine?

(6) Do I still love and want this person in my life, and if so, will a harsh confrontation on my part drive him back to the former lover?

Again, my advice is that you pray first, consider the issues, then pray again for direction in dealing with them. There is no simple solution, as this is not a simple problem. In fact, it's com-pounded, because you're hurting over the infidelity and the un-truth. But God is a healing specialist, whose resume includes pa-tients with marital success after adultery. And it's been my experi-ence that if you consult the Physician on your knees, He will gladly take and handle your case...but on His own schedule. Be patient.

50

Q. I'm in a church where the spiritual teaching is godly and on target, but the pastor clearly does not practice what he preaches as far as his own marriage is concerned. Should this affect whether or not I continue to hear him, or determine whether I remain a member of his church?

A. 2 Corinthians 5:16
Wherefore henceforth know we no man after the flesh...

THOUGHT

Make no mistake about it: if you've got a mind to live right, your minister's hypocrisy will affect how you hear him. For while the Scripture does tell us to "know no man after the flesh," your pastor is set before you to be a godly example, not to just preach godly topics. Seek God about how to proceed. He may just answer you by leading you to a new place of worship.

51

Q. I am a single woman who wants to one day be married. When dating, what qualifications or characteristics should I look for in a man in order to know whether or not he should be my spouse?

THOUGHT

First of all, be realistic. There is no such thing as "the perfect spouse," and if there are any major concerns present that you are not pleased with while dating, don't assume those things will change after marriage. Also, never marry based solely on vain qualifications or characteristics in any person. Be led of the Lord and never rush or allow yourself to be pressured into marriage. Marriage is honorable and pleasing to God, and "he that findeth a wife, findeth a good thing." (Proverbs 18:22) Apply godly principles and judgement in addition to any personal idiosyncrasies or ideas that you may have regarding your personal vision of what you would like your marriage to be.

52

Q. My husband tends to say and do things in front of company that I personally find embarrassing, especially when the jokes are at my expense. When I confronted him on it, he claimed that I've always been too serious and sensitive, and accused me of trying to change his fun-loving, outgoing personality. Am I unreasonable to want him to change that aspect of himself that wants to act a fool in public, and make me look like one, as well?

THOUGHT

Certainly not—what is unreasonable is the way he is treating you! Don't ask him anything. Tell him that you simply will not tolerate his lack of consideration and overriding of your feelings! Whether his bad behavior has to do with his personality,. or with the fact that he is totally insensitive to you. (the more likely of the two...), you must let him know that you can no longer afford him the luxury of self-expression at your expense. If you're as "serious" as he claims, use that no-nonsense quality to be firm with him, and he will be forced to give you the public and private respect that you deserve.

53

Q. My husband claims that I'm tight-fisted when it comes down to our personal finances, but I consider him to be too frivolous with money. How do we compromise?

THOUGHT

Very easily—get a budget. Take an assessment of the amount of funds coming into your household. Pay your bills. Pay your commitments to the Lord. Save. With what is left, allot yourselves a weekly or monthly allowance. Don't ask each other how theirs was spent.

54

Q. I married a man with incredibly strong family ties, and I can't seem to get him to have as much fun with me as he appears to have when visiting his parents or siblings. Is it ridiculous for me to be so concerned about this?

A. Matthew 19:5
For this cause shall a man leave father and mother, and shall cleave to his wife: and they twain shall be one flesh?

THOUGHT
   I don't think so. You are right to want your husband to enjoy your company as much as, and even more so than, he does his family's. If you are certain that it's not something you're doing (or not doing) to make him run for the comforts of home so happily and frequently, pray to find out what it is that you're dealing with. It could be there are emotional ties between your husband and his first family that are all too powerful. Is there spiritual warfare involved here that needs special attention? Ask God for insight into how to help your husband break these unhealthy bonds (if that is indeed what they are), so that he can reconnect them to you.

55

Q. The man I'm preparing to marry is having problems earning the respect of my three children from a past relationship,
because they see his presence as my betrayal of their father.
Since we are all going to be living together, how do I help
establish a comfortable arrangement where my kids are more
understanding of my need to remarry, and are accepting of
the new man in my life?

THOUGHT

This will take some time, plain and simple, so slow things
down. Don't force the relationship, and don't lose your children over it—it's not worth it. Children are a blessing from
God, and you'll have to answer to Him if you don't do right
by them, not if you don't ever remarry. Pray and have patience. God sees your need, but He knows your children's, as
well, and wants to see you put them first.

50

Q. My husband is a Christian man who is having problems breaking the cycle of domestic abuse established by his parents when he was a child. What can I do to affect immediate change in his life and behavior so he can stop hurting me and the children?

THOUGHT

Admitting his problem is the first step to overcoming it, but at the same time, he needs to stop blaming his present unacceptable, unmanly behavior on his past!

In many cases, I think it is merely a cop-out to say, "Since my dad beat on my mom, I can't help but beat on my wife." Though this may be true as it relates to generational curses and how our childhood environments influence our behavior in adulthood, the fact remains that if he is indeed a Christian, at some point during those times when he wants to raise his hand to strike you, some type of alarm or warning bell should go off in his heart and conscience to prevent him from being abusive again.

Have him ask himself the following question: "Do I love this woman to whom I am married, or do I hate or resent her in some way?" If there some hidden resentments toward you, he'll never be able to properly deal with the problem. It's been my observation that in many cases, a man has to like a woman first, then love her, then fall in love with her, and then like her all over again...

A short note to your husband:

If you love your wife, then, you will want to stop hurting her. And if you find that you don't love her, you need to remove yourself from her life, unless and until you find that you can abide with her and your children peaceably, without being abusive to them. Learn to apply the discipline of self-control to your life so that you can stop the violent behavior, and ask God for a complete and thorough deliverance.

57

Q. I'm a modern-day career woman in love with a man who has traditional ideas about marriage and family. Should I put my personal ambitions on hold for a short time to marry, become a housewife for, and raise the family of this man I so deeply care about?

THOUGHT

I really can't stress this point enough: Never do anything to get a person that you won't always be willing to do to keep them!

The question you must ask yourself is, "How much am I willing to give up for what I will receive?" If your answer is, for example, "Not my personal goals," then don't marry someone who will demand that you give up your personal goals — not even if they tell you it'll only be for a short time! Marriage is a commitment, and you want to start out in it pretty much the way you want to end up. And as a general rule, never allow yourself to be manipulated into giving up too much, ever! (What is that other individual going to give up? That's the question!)

58

Q. According to the Bible, we should forgive one another endlessly, but I think my spouse, who's had multiple affairs, is taking me and this particular passage of Scripture too far! Do I have to keep taking him back and putting off divorce, just because he apologizes every time?

A. Matthew 5:31-32
It hath been said, Whosoever shall put away his wife, let him give her a writing of divorcement: But I say unto you, That whosoever shall put away his wife, saving for the cause of fornication...

THOUGHT
Since you do have proof of your spouse's infidelity and you're clearly tired of his empty promises and apologizing, you are free to do as the Scripture says, and "put him away," or let him go. For him, the "seventy times seven" rule of forgiven is obsolete, because he's taken your kindness for weakness and, quite frankly, is putting your life in danger by being so promiscuous. May God grant you His peace in making and sticking to your decision to free yourself.

59

Q. I considered myself to be a happy and satisfied married woman, until recently, when I met through my professional circle a man to whom I feel an unshakable attraction. Since we work together every day and I can't avoid being around him, what can I do to contain myself, so that I don't get involved in a way that I'll later regret?

A. Proverbs 6:25
Lust not after her beauty in thine heart; neither let her take thee with her eyelids.

THOUGHT
Trust God and get another job, or ask Him to remove the man. Actually, you probably need to go the most expedient route, so let's go back to you trusting God for another job and getting out of there!

It's just a fact of life that each of us has somebody out there that we never need to meet, let alone get involved with, because they'll only ensnare us. This man, to tell you the truth, sounds like yours—but only in the sense that you need to flee from him, of course! So do it as soon as possible. God and your husband are depending on you to be strong enough to resist.

Q. My partner is an extremely attractive individual who gets constant attention from the opposite sex, not only because of how they look, but, I am convinced, because my mate encourages this attention from others through their flirtatious personality. Am I just being insecure, or do I have legitimate cause for concern?

THOUGHT

In this instance, the answer is both. There is no question that you are insecure. The issue is whether it is indeed your mate who's making you insecure.

Examine yourself to find out whether or not you're being too possessive and controlling, or if it's possible that you resent your partner's attractiveness. If so, at least part of the problem lies with you. This doesn't mean that your mate isn't too flirtatious, however. While they can't help that they're attractive, they can stop the flirting, if it's indeed what's going on. If you're giving them the proper time and attention, then there's no reason for it to go on.

Then if all is right on your part, confront your mate and have them make you certain of their devotion by declaring it, and by cutting out the unwise prancing and romancing!

Get your partner to make you secure; it's their job. There's no reason why you should have to doubt or wonder about their fondness for or faithfulness to you—and you alone.

61

Q. If polygamy is wrong, why is it that in biblical times, some of God's most favored men were allowed to have multiple, and even thousands, of wives?

A. 1 Corinthians 7:2
...Let every man have his own wife, and let every woman have her own husband.

THOUGHT
   Society is ever changing, and it did even in biblical times. For while the Hebrew law of the Old Testament may have allowed one man many women, as you can see from the Scripture above, by the New Testament era and the invent of Christianity, two-person relationships were being strongly encouraged. Even today, in countries such as Africa and India, where polygamy has been historically noted and commonly associated, the tradition is slowly but surely fading. The lesson is that what was good yesterday is sometimes spoiled tomorrow; polygamy is one of those such out-dated practices. (In most cases, when it is a man asking this question it's because he is having an extra-marital affairs...Most men can't handle one woman. What makes them think they can oblige two or three??)

62

Q. For years I have supported the pastorship of my husband, but now that I feel called to minister, I can't get him to support mine. He seems to want to remain the behind-the-scenes supporter in the church where I've always been, in full dedication to his ministry. How do I get him to acknowledge and respect that there is a call on my own life, without appearing to no longer be in subjection to him?

THOUGHT

In marriage, it is most unwise, and I'll even say that it's wrong, to do things and commit to things on behalf of your mate that you will not always remain faithful to. The most likely reason why your husband is not supporting you in this, your new calling, is because he's never had to do so before. All of what you've presented to him is rather foreign. It is somewhat understandable why he can't understand or is unwilling to accept that after all these years of you supporting and helping to build him up to where he is in ministry, you're now deciding to pursue your own.

It is an unfortunate fact, oftentimes, that after we have given years of our lives to another, and have finally gotten wise to the reality that our own needs, dreams, and individuality have to be attended to, the support we need is not reciprocated. Sometimes we allow things to work a certain way for so long in our relationships that change becomes unwelcome and very hard to bring about. My best advice to you, then, is to pray, pray, pray. Ask God to speak to you concerning the proper time to pursue that which He has given you, as well as how to peaceably execute your ministry so that it doesn't conflict with or negatively affect your husband's. Ask God to speak to your husband concerning you, and what you feel you must do for the Lord, so that the inevitable transition in your relationship and in his ministry will go as smoothly as possible.

03

Q. I am a young, single woman who, prior to my salvation, was always sexually active. Now that I am in the church and believe that it is a sin to fornicate, how do I properly handle my still-present desire for physical intimacy until I can find a husband?

A. 1 Corinthians 7:37
...He that standeth stedfast in his heart, having no necessity, but hath power over his own will, and so hath decreed in his heart that he will keep his virgin, doeth well.

THOUGHT

Through discipline. Salvation and deliverance are not always one and the same. You have the former, and need the latter, which can be achieved by your deliberate determination to live a disciplined lifestyle of abstinence. There's no easy way to do it, either, because discipline isn't easy, but it's something that as a dedicated believer you must do. At least until your change—which you hope is a husband—comes.

64

Q. Does every individual have a soul mate, and if so, is this the design of God or of nature? Could there possibly be more than one perfect person for some individuals? Finally, if for some reason one never meets up with that one individual who is ideal for them, is the course of their life somehow set off balance, causing them to live short of their intended destiny?

THOUGHT

This question has three parts, so I will answer it in like manner.

(1) Yes, I believe that every person does have a "soul mate," which is the design of both God and nature, because God is nature and nature is God.

(2) I absolutely believe that there can be more than one "perfect person" for some individuals, because successful relationships are based upon like backgrounds, things in common, attraction, and compatibility, and many people have all of these things in common with more than one person in the world. My suggestion, nevertheless, is that you stick with the person whom you considered "perfect" enough to marry, if at all possible, for this is the will of God. And if you haven't yet found that ideal someone, acknowledge God as a relationship establisher and builder and allow Him to lead and direct you to your perfect mate, so that you get it right the first time and won't have to look again.

(3) The course of one's life can be off-set if their best half is never found, but only if they base the success of their life upon relationships, which is a tragedy and a severe mistake. This may be hard for some of you to get, but there is more to life than marriage and relationships, so don't think the success of your life depends on them!

05

Q. My spouse appears to be resentful of the recent progress I've made in several areas of my life. While I've tried to include him in my success, he still tells me that he feels left out. How do I reassure my man that it's not my intention to leave him behind, but let him know that I can't quit achieving to accommodate his feelings?

THOUGHT

This sounds like a classic example of control in a relationship. To me, your mistake seems to be in trying to please someone who can't be pleased, or appeased! Since this is the case, there's no sense in continuing to waste your time trying to pacify your dependent spouse. Do continue to move on in your success, nevertheless, and remember that great people do great things, while nobodies do nothing!

Pray that God will work on his heart and that his spirit of jealousy over your success will be removed.

66

Q. During the down-times in marriage, which is less risky: to deal with heavy, heated issues at the time that they arise, when feelings are sensitive, and attitudes sour, and partners inevitably say hurtful things they later regret; or to handle touchy subjects after some time has lapsed, giving space to the possibility that negative feelings have festered and reached a boiling point?

A. Ephesians 4:26

Be ye angry and sin not: Let not the sun go down upon your wrath...

THOUGHT

Sometime ago, I visited Jamaica, West Indies, as an assigned missionary. While there, I was struck by a rather meaningful phrase that the locals had coined: "Don't eat rice while it's hot."

This is to say that if you touch the issue when it is too heated, it will inevitably burn you! Leave it alone until things have "cooled" down, and even afterward, seek God for the right time to again approach the subject. It may be that you can avoid both the initial argument and the later explosion, because again, timing is everything.

67

Q. I think it is extremely petty and closed-minded of my husband to be upset that I am now earning more money than him. How can I help him be less sensitive about the fact that he is no longer the primary breadwinner?

THOUGHT

You can start by telling him to get a better job, since he's into competition! Your husband, ma'am, sounds like a little boy with a man's ego: he's got a lot of catching up to do!

While I realize that being chief provider in the household is important to a lot of men, it's also a rather outdated way of looking at the world—the modern world. Men who have these controlling, traditionalist mentalities really need to get with it. If he really cared about your feelings or your achievement, he would see your success as his, especially since the two of you are supposed to be "one flesh." Tell him to be happy for you, be looking for better employment, or be quiet!

68

Q. What is the proper interpretation of the Scripture that speaks of being "unequally yoked with unbelievers"?

A. 2 Corinthians 6:14
Be ye not unequally yoked together with unbelievers: for what fellowship hath righteousness with unrighteousness? and what communion hath light with darkness?

THOUGHT

The emphasis of this Scripture is on the yoke, not the relationship with the unbeliever. This fact suggests that there can be imbalance and inequality in all areas of a "yoking," or relationship, and this off-setting is due to the incompatibility of unsuccessful couples.

For persons planning to spend the rest of their lives with someone, I suggest that there be multiple commonalities between the two of you. The first of which, for Christian singles, should be salvation and a love for Jesus Christ. When two people who come together are God-fearing and have fundamental likes, dislikes, and experiences in common, they are better able to stay with each other when the seasons of marriage inevitably change, and the passion has temporarily gone.

69

Q. What is the number one cause of marital breakups?

THOUGHT
   Lack of communication and financial instability.

   So talk and go to work!

70

Q. Since falling in love can be deceiving, as it makes one emotionally vulnerable, how does one distinguish the sensation of passion from that of true love, to ensure that they marry for the right reason?

THOUGHT

You are right to want to know the difference between the two, but unfortunately, the answer is not exactly one I can provide you through clear definition. I could look up both of these emotions for you and relay to you what the dictionary says, but I'd rather not. This is because both passion and love are feelings, and they are experienced on different levels and on an individual basis. And while the Bible speaks heavily concerning love, the spiritual variety (always willing the good of the other person) is what it typically refers to, and your question clearly concerns the romantic.

We can all experience passion frequently, but from what I've heard and experienced, true love is not as commonly found. Supposedly, it is rare and so unique that it is evidenced only by the behavior of the affected individual. It's so exclusive, in fact, that the only way to interpret or recognize it is to "know" that it is indeed what's happening to you. It's probably safe to say, then, that if you find yourself questioning whether or not it's there, more than likely, it isn't.

71

Q. The Scripture tells us that "the eyes of man are never satisfied." Does this mean that I shouldn't be furious with my man if and when he looks at other women?

THOUGHT

The Scripture also tells us, "If thine eye offend thee, pluck it out," so absolutely not. You should be furious with him if you catch his gaze varying from yours! Life and marriage are a discipline, and mutual respect is crucial to the longevity of your relationship. If you demand respect, he will love you more.

72

Q. Before I met my husband, I shared with another wonderful man a great platonic friendship. Now that I am married, am I somehow obligated to end my conversation and comraderie with this man that I knew first, even if my husband doesn't object to our closeness?

A. Genesis 3:13
And the Lord God said unto the woman, What is this that thou hast done? And the woman said, The serpent beguiled me, and I did eat.

THOUGHT

The scripture verse was chosen not to suggest that your platonic friend is a snake, but to alert you to the possibility and likelihood that your relationship with him will poison your marriage!

Get rid of him. It matters not if your husband has no objection to the friendship. Break off your friendship with him. You owe it to your husband, yourself, and your friend, who doesn't deserve to be lead down a potentially romantic path with a married woman. You need to make clear your single-minded commitment to the single marriage relationship to which you have avowed yourself.

There's an old rap song whose revelatory lyrics describe an unfaithful partner in relationship. "You, you've got what I need. But you say he's just a friend. You say he's just a friend," the betrayed lover laments. The very probable outcome of your situation is illustrated by these potent words, and your husband will eventually be the one singing them! Quit this business of having one marriage in two locations. While your passion may be at home with your husband, your emotional and psychological support are coming from across the street. Before you know it, all of you will have moved to a different block! It's the Eve and the Serpent Syndrome, hands down, and you're only moments away from biting the forbidden fruit!

73

Q. I am an incest and emotional abuse survivor, still bearing serious emotional scars that are preventing me from getting close to any man. For this I am seeking counseling, because I very much want to be married, but I fear that even after therapy and prayer, I'll never be completely whole. I'm worried that, in the end, I will ultimately prove dissatisfying to my future mate. Is there any real hope for me for a successful relationship?

A. 1 John 4:18
There is no fear in love; but perfect love casteth out fear: because fear hath torment. He that feareth is not made perfect in love.

THOUGHT

No, there isn't any real hope for you for a successful relationship...if you don't let go of fear. Your very question is full of the spirit of fear. You must let it go.

Doubt is understandable as a natural, human emotion, and what you have gone through is enough to make anyone wonder about the future possibilities. But at the same time, fear and doubt are ungodly, and it'll take God to deliver you from this questioning, wondering, disbelieving spirit that He doesn't approve of. Be comforted by the knowledge that you are not alone. Others have gone through similar ordeals and have overcome. What's more, God is there with you, and He sees your pain and confusion. As you seek a closer walk with Him, He will help you develop positive, successful relationships with others.

74

Q. According to the Apostle Paul, "It is good for a man not to touch a woman." What exactly is meant by this passage of Scripture, and does it apply to women relating to men, as well?

A. 1 Corinthians 7:1
Now concerning the things whereof ye wrote unto me: It is good for a man not to touch a woman.

THOUGHT

In this particular Scriptural text, I believe that Paul was advising Christian individuals against having intimate relations before marriage. Though the address is made to men, the apostle speaks to women, as well—"it is good for a man not to touch a woman"—meaning it is good for all mankind to refrain from intimate involvement with the opposite sex before making the permanent, legal commitment. This truth is made plain in the verse that follows (1 Cor. 7:2): "Nevertheless, to avoid fornication, let every man have his own wife, and let every woman have her own husband."

75

Q. I am an elderly widow who has discovered that after years of being alone, I am actually lonely. Is this reason enough for me to consider marrying again?

THOUGHT

Certainly. Marriage is a blessing of companionship, fellowship, and support, which people in all walks and stages of life need. Seek God, and your Mr. Right will surely come.

76

Q. My husband has some highly sensitive areas in his life that I feel he could experience healing in, if he would only open himself up to discussing them. Should I gently nudge him to address these issues with me, through which I would assure him of my unconditional love and support, or do I allow him to hold his feelings in until he thinks he is ready to confront them, which could mean never?

THOUGHT

This question is not one that I am able to easily answer, simply because I don't know your mate. But you do. It is not up to me, then, to advise you on how to address delicate issues with your spouse, because only you really know the type of individual they are, and what will and will not work concerning them. The duty lies, again, with you.

Of course, if you're asking me for such advice, then perhaps you really don't know your companion, in which case I am able to advise you a little. Get to know them. For if you don't know the fundamentals of who they are, then there's no way you can help heal their sore spots.

77

Q. My marriage partner has expressed interest in exploring certain intimate activities with which the two of us have never previously experimented. To me, however, such acts are taboo. How do we compromise without depriving each other?

THOUGHT

Now hold on a minute, here now. Now there are a lot of issues I don't mind discussing, and plenty of things I don't mind helping folks with, but this question is not one of them! I can't give y'all EVERYTHING!

Some intimate concerns are better left to one's self...they need to be figured out, or something, privately. My advice is that you go to a church somewhere and get under some timely teaching! Then if you still have questions, ask your pastor! Because I won't be authorizing anyone to unleash the spirit of perversion in their bedroom, nor any other spirit onto the pages of this book!

So Questioner, when you address your own minister with this particular concern, be sure to write me and tell what his or her answer was! Also, don't forget to include your full name, so that I may place you on the altar!

Q. I have a great relationship with the young man I am currently seeing, but I'm having a slight problem with his public
displays of affection. While it is common knowledge in the
church and community that we are "seeing" each other, and
I don't mind kissing him in private, I somehow feel it is inap-
propriate for us to kiss and hold too much in public, since we
are not actually married. Is this right, or am I just being hypo-
critical?

THOUGHT

It sounds to me as though you are a very respectable
young lady, and I advise you not to compromise your convictions. I think you are very right—there is no reason, regardless of how passionate we feel, for any of us to expose
our private lives to the public. Socially speaking, it's pretty
tacky, and spiritually speaking, it's indecent and out of order.

This is not to say that when you are married, you can't
be openly affectionate with your mate, but there are limits
on how that affection is to be demonstrated in the of company strangers. Also, as the two of you are unmarried Christians, you need to be mindful that you don't give the impression of doing what married folks do. Inform your mate that
intimacy can be sacred, but that it's up to the two of you to
guard it and keep it holy.

79

Q. There's a still-intact soul tie between me and a woman with whom I shared a long, intense, intimate relationship previous to my conversion. While I feel myself getting over her, she is still clearly obsessed with me and won't let me go. Since trying to let her down gently hasn't worked, how do I make this girl understand that we really are through, without totally hurting her feelings?

THOUGHT

Unfortunately, there is no way for you to get the word of finality across, except very firmly. You must be up-front with her and tell her, simply, to *leave you alone*!

What I have prescribed for you—a very direct and decided approach—will not work for you, however, if what you told me about you getting over is not true. Get over her. Don't further hinder your spiritual growth and progress by encouraging the haunting of an old but familiar spirit. Indeed, you sounded when describing your relationship with this woman as a soul tie still tied, but you must untie it! If you don't, and she senses that she still has a bit of a hold on you, she will keep tugging at your heart strings until you are again one with her. But you keep pulling the other way. And if all else fails, get The Law to intervene and have them apply their own awesome powers of persuasion!

Q. My husband left me for another woman in our church, and I'm now finding it impossible to get along with her. Am I at fault for no longer liking this woman, and how do I deal with my feelings of resentment toward both her and my ex-husband?

THOUGHT

Here is a classic case of bad leadership. No pastor should encourage divorce and remarriage within the same church. In fact, church leaders ought to discourage such things! It all makes for bad church relations, and it sets a poor example for the unsaved community. (See Question 30.)

While we Christians would like to think that as Christ-like, spiritual beings, we can handle anything, the truth is that we are still flesh. The natural reality is that when trying times and devastating incidents affect our lives, we can't always control our emotions and actions, or pray our negative feelings away. Therefore, I sympathize with you, ma'am, and can understand your feelings of resentment. But the only way that I can see these angry emotions leaving is if you leave the church. Unless your ex-husband and his new wife somehow decide to go, there's probably no hope of peace for you in that highly sensitive, potentially hostile environment. For not only will you be hurt and angry every time you see these two people together, or apart, but your worship itself will be hindered by your thoughts concerning them. So talk to your pastor, if you are able, and seek the direction of God concerning where you can start fellowshiping anew.

81

Q. My partner and I are not addicted to pornographic movies and magazines, but we do enjoy them. Is our interest in such material unchristian?

A. Romans 1:21
Because that, when they knew God, they glorified him not as God, neither were thankful; but became vain in their imaginations, and their foolish heart was darkened.

THOUGHT

Yes. Pornography is "vain imagination." Even if you are not yet "addicted," you are certainly standing in the doorway of sexual addiction, not to mention, embracing the spirit of Perversion.

What you consider to be the no-harm viewing of others' nakedness and intimate activity is really an abomination to the Lord. Even society teaches us that dirty books, movies, magazines, and other such perverted paraphernalia are something to be ashamed of, and at least covered up and done in hush-hush secrecy. How much more shame, then, before the holy God?

If the two of you can see the error of your way and want to change, confession—the process of which you have begun by your questioning—is the first step. Then, after repentance, counseling, should you seek it, will usher in your total deliverance.

82

Q. The person to whom I am married has "admitted to having homosexual urges." Should I consider leaving him, or do I need to wait and see if he actually act upon these impulses, or even try to find out whether he already has?

A. 1 Corinthians 6:9
Know ye not that the unrighteous shall not inherit the kingdom of God? Be not deceived: neither fornicators, nor idolaters, nor adulterers, nor effeminate...

THOUGHT

All of the above. The Bible tells us, "In all thy getting, get understanding," so you need find out from your mate what exactly is going on, and then make some crucial decisions.

Homosexuality is an abomination to God (See Question 32). It is a sin that absolutely cannot be tolerated, particularly in this, the age of AIDS and other deadly sexual diseases. So protect yourself in all areas and seek God for a solution to your situation, if indeed the "urges" of your mate develop into permanent desires or actual tendencies.

If not, know that reconciliation and forgiveness should be the order of the day in any Christian's life. Communicate to your spouse your concerns, hear them out, and determine together what is to be the future of your relationship.

83

Q. For many years now, I've been "shacking up," so to speak, with the man that I love, and together with our children, we've been living happily as if we were husband and wife. Now that I've accepted Christ into my life, however, I feel that it is important for us to become officially married and have our union legalized, but my partner can't see the necessity of a mere ceremony, since we've already been living as a committed couple. What, then, should I do about the image of our relationship?

A. Hebrews 13:4; 2 Corinthians 5:17
Marriage is honourable in all, and the bed undefiled: but whoremongers and adulterers God will judge. Therefore if any man be in Christ, he is a new creature: old things are passed away; behold, all things are become new

THOUGHT

Really, you have no Christian choice but to leave this man, until he comes to the knowledge of God. Your new commitment to your Heavenly Father is too strong and too sacred for you to stay unlawfully committed to this man and the "old" way. Pray for your partner, that he, too, will surrender his life to the will of God, but let him know what the ultimatum is: either marriage or permanent separation.

84

Q. Although he is not abusive, my husband has such a forceful and domineering way about him that I sometimes have problems feeling like a grown-up in his presence. At times, in fact, he almost becomes like a father figure to me, because he gives me constant advice, expects me to obey it, and is always offering me correction. How do I begin to assert some authority of my own in this relationship, so that I feel less like my husband's subject, and more like his equal?

THOUGHT

In your marriage relationship there appears to be clear evidence of spiritual warfare, possibly even witchcraft. Domination, intimidation, manipulation, and control are all signs of the witching spirit, and these are what you have described to me as being dealt out by your husband.

Fortunately, this is a spirit and curse that can be broken and demolished through the powers of prayer and fasting. Seek the Lord for some personal time alone to yourself, where you can be temporarily free from your husband's oppressive rule, and get close to God for protection. Search for Scriptures to properly appropriate for this spiritual war—for war is indeed what it is—dress up in your spiritual war clothes and realize that the battle is on! Because it is the Lord's, nevertheless, victory is a sure thing, and we win!

85

Q. To what extent should illegitimate children born outside of the current marriage relationship be involved in that union?

A. Genesis 21:10
Wherefore she said unto Abraham, Cast out this bondwoman and her son: for the son of this bondwoman shall not be heir with my son, even with Isaac.

THOUGHT

In many instances, illegitimate children bring a curse upon the marriage relationship. It is important to understand that there are two separate units abiding within a typical household: the marriage and the family. According to biblical principle, the illegitimate child is a part of neither.

In modern relationships, children born outside of the current marriage union are no longer an exception. When things are not handled properly, these children often act and/or are treated as household misfits, upsetting the family peace by being the frequent source of arguments, negative feelings, and economical strain. This is the why Sarah, wife of Abraham, ordered her husband to get his unlawful son, Ishmael, out of her house!

On the other hand, if a husband and wife desire to include the child born out of wedlock as an active member of the family, or choose to establish a regular visitation schedule with the child, as long as such plans are accompanied by prayer and some spiritual guidance, things need not be problematic. Just remember that the marriage and family are indeed separate entities, so that the relationship between you and your spouse should never be adversely affected by issues involving your children, illegitimate or otherwise.

86

Q. My husband and I are continually having babies. If the Bible says "be fruitful and multiply," is it a sin to use birth control?

A. Hosea 4:6
My people are destroyed for a lack of knowledge: because thou hast rejected knowledge...

THOUGHT

The issue presented in this question is one to which much controversy is attached. In my opinion, birth control is a blessing. It has nothing to do with abortion, as some try to argue, but everything to do with control, as its name suggests. This control is one that allows you to plan and build a stable, successful family unit, which is the will of God.

If you notice, preparation usually proceeds natural and spiritual blessings. Before they actually conceived, God spoke to the biblical matriarchs Mary, Sarah, and Elizabeth, announcing to them the blessed births of their baby boys ahead of time, in order that they might be prepared.

If you don't subscribe to the type of family planning and preparation that birth control allows you, then hold fast to your personal conviction and don't use it; neither should you judge others who do. On the other hand, if it's a method of control that you do find beneficial to your family, use it without condemning yourself.

87

Q. I was a sinner when I married and divorced, now I am saved. Am I allowed to remarry?

A. 2 Corinthians 5:17
Therefore if any man be in Christ, he is a new creature: old things are passed away; behold, all things are become new.

THOUGHT

This is one of those questions where the answer varies, depending on which Christian you ask. There are those orthodox believers who simply don't accept divorce as the official severing of the marital tie. Those who hold this view believe that once you marry an individual, you are married to that person until you or they die.

But Jesus himself said that because of adultry, divorce is sometimes necessary and appropriate, and Scripture assures us that once the legal separation is made, you are no longer bound. If you're not bound, then you are free. Free to remarry, as well as determine whether you believe you mustn't remarry, because you are still convinced of the validity of your original marriage union.

This is a personal call. Seek God for the spiritual answer that will provide you a clear, sure solution to your romantic condition.

88

Q. Who has the last say, the husband or the wife?

A. Ephesians 5:21
Submitting yourselves one to another in the fear of God.

THOUGHT

In a day and time when preachers are using the pulpit as a platform to bully and brow-beat women into unquestioned acquiescence to the will of men, the Bible breathes a breath of fresh air. It advocates mutual submission.

Submission doesn't have a potentate. It's not a dictatorship, but rather includes a shared throne of authority. God did place the male at the head of the household, but the female, his wife, was meant to reign alongside him.

According to the Bible, the woman is a "help meet" for the man, one who helps him meet the family's obligations, helps him meet the bills, helps him meet their mutual goals. Men, it is time for us to return to humbling ourselves and being ministered to through our wive's innate ministries of helps.

Let us stop trying to have absolute rule and help them by supporting their ideas, their assertions, and their goals as we peacefully lay down the wound-inflicting weaponry of male chauvinism and unregulated ego.

Q. Why are there so many divorces and unhappy marriages within the body of Christ?

A. Psalms 1:1
Blessed is the man that walketh not in the counsel of the ungodly...

THOUGHT

When Christian people seek counsel from ungodly sources, curses are inevitably brought into their lives. The unholy guidance and advice of physics, astrologers, motivational speakers, self-help groups, and new-age institutions have caused the blessings of God to be revoked from the marriages and relationships of those people who claim to believe on Jesus, but put their faith in men of Satanic spirit.

It is for this reason, along with Christian couples' growing intolerance for one another and unwillingness to stick by choices made that there is rampant dissatisfaction and fruitlessness in our romantic unions. I also believe that the advice of the Apostle Paul—"it is better to marry than to burn"—has been perverted in the minds of certain believers by the Enemy. Many members of the Body of Christ are getting married for the sole purpose of fulfilling sexual desire. Marriage wasn't instituted by God for the legalizing of sex, however, and marriages based exclusively upon physical passion and attraction will inevitably grow cold.

It is my conviction that if we return to abiding by the moral laws of righteousness, and reinstitute the most essential of the traditional values of the church into our lives, the favor of God will shine once again upon us, blessing and brightening both our spiritual walks and our natural relationships.

90

Q. My husband is a minister who's dedicated to the Body of Christ but neglectful of his family. How do I bring this to his attention?

A.1 Timothy 5:8
But if any provide not for his own, and specially for those of his own house, he hath denied the faith and is worse than an infidel.

THOUGHT

Some time ago, when I was very much like the husband described in the above question, my spiritual father told me to "get alone with the Lord." You see, I had become so involved with the work of God that I was falling out of the will of God, and this was becoming obvious to those around me. In order to recover my neglected family and my focus, then, I had to reapproach the throne of grace and have God redirect my attention to what really mattered and was actually required of me.

Many ministers today are in similar predicaments: they are zealous, sincere, and dedicated to their divine appointings and anointings, but they are out of the will of Him who called them in the first place, because of areas left unattended, and family is often the first obligation to go lacking.

No question about it, brethren, these things ought not be. The family is at the heart of God, and a strong family is the healthy heartbeat of the properly regulated church. Ministry is not just in the strolling of the pulpit but includes the rewarding task of ruling well one's household. This means the unceasing provision of economic stability, love and support, chastisement and correction, direction and guidance, conversation and companionship, and especially important, fun.

To the wives of Christian men everywhere: whether your husband is a high-ranking bishop on the platform, or a faithful bench-warmer in the pews, his first obligation is to his family. If he is neglectful of you and the children, use the Word of God to bring his duty and his oversight to his attention. As a true child of God, he will certainly repent, turn, and mend his ways; sincere hearts always do.

91

Q. I love my husband but hate the fact that his mother is ruling our household. What should I do?

A. Matthew 19:5
...For this cause shall a man leave his father and mother, and shall cleave to his wife: and they twain shall be one flesh...

THOUGHT

Many parents don't realize it, but there must be a cutting away of two umbilical cords that extend from themselves to their children. The first is the obvious physical cord, severed automatically after the child is born, and the second is the emotional tie, to be broken years later, when that child has found a mate with whom to make a new, permanent connection. This does not mean that the parents and child can no longer love and communicate with one another, but that the bonds of control and influence that stretch between them were intended by God to be broken and reattached elsewhere.

That elsewhere, again, is to the spouse. In many instances, however, too-involved and too-controlling parents prevent the proper detachment and reattachment from ever occurring, because they selfishly refuse to relinquish the emotional ties. Usually, this tragedy plays out in the development of a tumultuous, resentful relationship between a new wife and her husband's mother, or between a husband and his wife's mother, mainly because mothers-in-law are female, and females generally make and have difficulty breaking the strong emotional and psychological connections between them and those they love. In spite of science and gender, nevertheless, the Bible is clear on what the order of things ought to be and commands husbands and wives to rediscover the nurture and support that once came from mother and father, within the loving relationship with their spouses.

To the wife asking this question, then, the doing, or rather undoing, of your mother-in-law's stronghold on your home will be mainly up to your spouse. If his mother hasn't met her obligation to free him, it is still his duty to "leave" his mother and "cleave" to his wife. Tell him to initiate this most necessary separation, and if he's too attached, himself, and is unwilling, seek God for further assistance in handling the situation.

92

Q. I want to be married, but am reluctant to give up my successful, independent lifestyle. Is it possible for me to have a husband and retain my self-sufficiency?

A. 1 Corinthians 7:7-9
I say therefore to the unmarried and widows, It is good for them if they abide [unmarried]. But if they cannot contain, let them marry: for it is better to marry than to burn.

THOUGHT

The marriage issue can be complex for single women who've already provided for themselves the most fundamental of the elements that make marriage attractive to women: economic stability. Whether you like my saying so or not, the nature of a female, as designed by God, is to seek natural provisions from men, though modern society has evolved and made exceptional all of us. This means that, typically, when a woman has education, a fulfilling career, personal goals, and healthy esteem, she is less likely to see the "need" in her life for a man. Worldly success makes such a woman independent in mind and spirit, and excludes her from the common feminine need for a physical caretaker.

Nevertheless, the truth is that women also need emotional provision, which money can't buy nor success secure. So for professional single ladies who are Christian, the attractiveness of marriage primarily involves the missing components of companionship and sexual intimacy. For the independent woman who finds that, in addition to her career, she needs these missing elements in her life for total fulfillment, discipline then becomes key. Without question, getting used to a second voice of authority in the household requires discipline. Acting in the better interest of two, and not just one, requires discipline. Being humble and submissive when such is in order requires discipline. And learning dedication and commitment, virtues essential to the sustaining of any marriage relationship, will certainly take discipline.

In a nutshell, marriage is a commitment. None of this is not to say that your future husband won't be supportive of your career and ambitions—the two of you would need to work out all of the important details before actually tying the knot—but simply that there is a certain level of discipline, as well as a certain loss of independence, that being successfully married will demand of you. If the relationship is right for you, however, the "demands" won't be strenuous, but rather, you'll see them as necessary and worthy. The fact of the matter is that when honor and commitment are there, and both partners are doing their parts, marriage is a blessing.

Q. I married a man, only to recently find out that he is still legally married to someone else! Am I no longer his wife?

A. Matthew 5:32
But I say unto you, That whosoever shall put away his wife, saving for the cause of fornication, causeth her to commit adultery: and whosoever shall marry her that is divorced committeth adultery.

THOUGHT

No getting around it, yours is a cut-and-dried case of adultery. It is most unfortunate that the truth of your husband's marital status was kept hidden from you, but ignorance of the law is no excuse, and the illegality of your union with this man remains.

The Bible commands that when we hear the truth, we are to walk therein. This means that because you are a believer, in order to be restored to the favor of God, you must let your "husband" go. Do so, then—immediately—and repent for the adulterous relationship. Afterward, seek God. He will comfort your loss, heal your heart, and give you peace of mind.

94

Q. God showed me my husband, but he's married. Is this possible?

A. Exodus 20:17
Thou shalt not covet thy neighbour's house, thou shalt not covet thy neighbour's wife...

THOUGHT

It's a sad that the emphasis being placed upon marriage in the church today causes many single women to become obsessed with the hope and desire to tie the knot with someone. Anyone. And through this unhealthy obsession, Satan is steadily bringing about mass deception.

Disguising himself as an angel of light, foul-mouthed Lucifer is imitating the sacred voice of God and leading many believers—female and male—into covetousness and unsanctioned romantic attractions. Get this straight: God is not in the business of breaking up households and marriages and giving parts of them—or partners in them—to outsiders. Close your ears to Satan's seductive lies, and quit entertaining his lewd suggestions.

Secondly, marrying is not a commandment of God, nor is it a necessity; rather, it's a privilege. It's not something you're required to do, but if it's what you desire, you need to find out what it requires of you. Happy unions are shared between two individuals of like interests and passions, who are compatible personality-wise and are committed to the institution of marriage. So if you desire to be in relationship, allow God to lead you to that individual who is ideal for you. Make sure that it is Him directing you to that person to whom you're feeling attracted, and that the two of you have multiple things in common—the least of which shouldn't be your unmarried status!

Q. I've been in a relationship for quite some time now and things are going fine. Why should I get married?

A. 1 Corinthians 7:2
Nevertheless, to avoid fornication, let every man have his own wife, and let every woman have her own husband.

THOUGHT

Long-lasting courtships have become tolerated in Christendom today, but I consider them to be very dangerous. As any can see, fornication, diseases, and out-of-wedlock pregnancies are all too common, both outside of the church community and within. I see this as evidence that folks are playing around for too long with the fire of passion and are inevitably getting burnt!

But according to the Scriptures, marrying is better than burning. I am convinced that the flames of fornication are indeed avoidable if we would all just do as God's Word commands. Courtships and romantic relationships are really just unofficial marriages, anyway, and if you're in one for too long, the temptation becomes extremely great to start enjoying the sexual benefits of the institution, without the actual commitment thereof.

So don't tease yourself. If you've been in relationship for a while, and all is going well, you've probably come upon a person with whom you could spend even more time after you've made a public vow of commitment. If you are unsure, or know that individual is not for you, or don't think marriage is for you, end it. And in the future, don't waste time by remaining with someone whom you know you absolutely could not abide with permanently, or on casual dating, when you realize that you are not the marrying type.

96

Q. I'm a young "today's" woman, in hot pursuit of my Mr. Right. What does the Bible say about my proposing to him, when I find him?

A. Proverbs 18:22
Whoso findeth a wife findeth a good thing, and obtaineth favor of the Lord.

THOUGHT

I know that you just finished reading it, but if you will, please do take another careful look at the Scripture printed above....Have you done it? Good.

Now notice that the Word says "whoso findeth a wife"—not "whoso findeth a husband"—findeth a good thing. As a Bible-believing Christian and a traditional man, I am very much inclined to believe this.

Personally, I feel that it is out of order—the order of nature, the order of God, and that of more traditional society—for women to chase men. On the contrary, it is more natural for the man to pursue the woman, which is why the Scripture above makes reference only to whoever would be finding a wife, which is the man.

I believe that present-day men still enjoy practicing old-fashioned chivalry—the buying of dinner, the opening of doors, and the making of provisions for wife and family—when it comes to romance, and that most women still enjoy the treatment. This doesn't mean, however, that as a young lady desirous of permanent companionship, you shouldn't position yourself—in the proper, ladylike attire, with a positive, pleasant attitude, and within the right circles and environments—to have your Mr. Right find you. In fact, to discourage you from your hot pursuit, I will encourage you to do this: get in proper place and position.

Again, there are two ways for you to go about this. The first is to develop patience and faith in God, an attitude where you will allow your future mate to discover and propose to you when the time comes. Secondly, it is important that you abide where and how you don't mind being "found," meaning that you need to prepare yourself mentally, spiritually, and physically for companionship, as well as make sure that your environment, if not a sound one, does not dictate your relationship possibilities.

If you change your perspective on relationships, then, as well as the physical location, if necessary, from whence your companionship choices are coming, you will attract to yourself the best man for you. Only then could you say your Mr. Right had been gotten the right way.

97

Q. Is it true that a man's attraction to a woman, at least when he first meets her, is mostly physical?

THOUGHT

You must be a woman to ask this question. The answer is yes. Men generally do tend to go by and go after what they see, especially as it pertains to the opposite sex. It's just one of those laws of nature.

A man who is a womanizer, or one who is not serious about committed relationship, typically will determine that he likes a girl based upon his physical attraction to her. He will then use whatever and as many tactics necessary to seduce her. After he has conquered this woman sexually, then he will take a look at who she really is. After discovering that he doesn't like her personality, or who she is intellectually, or her emotionalism, he'll lose interest and leave. But he did appreciate the intimate encounter, of course!

Certainly, this is not the way Christian men ought to behave. Those who do fornicate and use women in this manner will pay natural and spiritual consequences. But by the same token, saved men are flesh-and-blood beings, and they, too, are generally drawn to females based upon their outward appearances or a physical attraction. And this is not necessarily bad or wrong. It just means that ladies need to beware of men who really mean them no good. You need to be aware of the fact that just because a man first likes them for who they are on the outside doesn't mean that he won't soon appreciate who they are inside.

98

Q. Is love a stipulation for successful marriage, or can two people get married and/or remain together without it?

A. Ephesians 5:25
Husbands, love your wives, even as Christ also loved the church, and gave himself for it...

THOUGHT

It's a fact that different people define "love" as different things. What some would consider passion, or obsession, or infatuation, or like, or attraction, or even dependency, those experiencing these emotions might actually call them love.

My suggestion would be that you love and be in love with your partner, however the two of you can healthily define this controversial emotion. But before you establish a permanent relationship, make sure you also like each other and have things in common. Not every person that we love is someone we are able or willing to live with. This proves to us the validity of the fact that the key component to successful marriage, more so than love, like, things in common, and any other of the relationship staples, is old-fashioned commitment.

99

Q. Supposedly, a lot of men are attracted to, and choose for wives, women who remind them of their own mothers. Why is this so?

THOUGHT

It is true that a significant number of males find attractive, and eventually marry, women who are similar to their mothers. The reasons behind this are generally very healthy. It's no secret that mothers are typically the most visible figures in the home. They are the primary role models to children and tend to have greater and more lasting influence in the lives of their offspring. It makes sense, then, that when men search for their "ideal" woman, they look for those traits and characteristics present in the first and most important woman in their lives — Mom. This same form of mate selection can be true for women who idolized their fathers.

Of course, there are many exceptions to this rule, because not everybody's mother — or father — was someone to emulate. In some case because of emotional resentment, some individuals may go about deliberately choosing partners unlike their parents. There are also situations where psychological tragedy occurs, and individuals who've been strongly impacted by the negative influence of their parents will gravitate toward and have relationships with persons who are mean, abusive, unsupportive, or neglectful as the parent they despise. Because the pattern is deep-rooted, they sometimes enter the same types of relationships over and over again, even when they know such persons are not good for them. In such cases, the mind-healing power of God is needed to come in and break the binding authority of a generational curse.

Q. Is the gender characterizing really accurate that says that women are more suited to domesticity and the raising of children, and men to social climbing and being breadwinners, or are these mostly just stereotypes?

THOUGHT

I would have to say that most gender characterizing is stereotypical, but that stereotypes often do have a bit of merit. In other words, stereotypes don't just appear from nowhere, regardless of how ignorantly or inaccurately they may be. Many women are better suited to a domestic existence than are most males, and likewise, most men are a bit more driven to be career achievers and natural providers than most women.

But again, the reverse is also true. For even as we speak, modern society is changing the way we view men and women, how we categorize them, and how we define what their roles are. Who each of us becomes is almost totally dependent upon the environment in which we are raised, how our mentalities are nurtured and develop, and how society dictates what we must do to survive. For example, particularly in America, there is a growing abundance of mom-like dads, and dad-like moms. This plainly illustrates to us the necessity of role reversal, and hints to us that even the gender stereotypes, themselves, will be transforming.

Personally, I don't see that there is anything inherently wrong with the way men and women are changing, as long as our sexuality, and what is essential to gender character, remains true to nature. Christians ought to remain true to their spiritual calling and remain steadfast in the place, position, and duty to the God Who Never Changes.

101

Q. Whenever I attempt to engage my wife in discussion about what it is that makes women tick, instead of her taking me seriously and giving me direct answers, she avoids my questions and conversation. But then she has no problem spending hours on the phone with one of her friends in unadulterated "girl talk"! Since I am truly interested in the psychology of women and am tired of ineffectual eavesdropping, what can I do to learn more about the fascinating subject of females?

THOUGHT

Evidently, your wife is a tried-and-true member of the FBI—the Female Bonding Institute—and probably enjoys teasing you with what, by nature, you were not intended to be a part of. There are some basic strategies, however, that you can easily employ to enter the exclusive ranks of the club for women only, in order to learn more about who these special creatures really are...

First, stop openly hounding your wife for clues and take time to silently observe her. Watch what she does and learn who she is—emotionally, mentally, spiritually, psychologically, physically—and become sensitive to her sensitivities and protective of her femininity. If you look and listen with love, you will undoubtedly learn.

Next, compare the mental notes you've gathered on your wife to those lessons life experience has taught you, as relating to previous women in your life, and discover what are the generalities, commonalities, and peculiarities between and among females.

You also need to read, so I suggest you consult the Word of God, where there's plenty to be found on relationships and female character.

George G. Bloomer

101 Questions Women Ask About Relationships

Other Books from Pneuma Life Publishing

WITCHCRAFT IN THE PEWS, George Bloomer
OPPRESSIONLESS, George Bloomer
WHEN LOVING YOU IS WRONG,
BUT I WANT TO BE RIGHT, George Bloomer
ANOINTING FALL ON ME, T.D. Jakes
WHY? BECAUSE YOU ARE ANOINTED, T.D. Jakes
THE HARVEST, T.D. Jakes
HELP ME, I'VE FALLEN, T.D. Jakes
WATER IN THE WILDERNESS, T.D. Jakes
BECOMING A LEADER, Myles Munroe
SEASONS OF CHANGE, Myles Munroe
SEX 101, Myles Munroe & Dave Burrows
MYLES MUNROE ON LEADERSHIP
HUSBAND 101 - EVERYTHING YOUR WIFE WISHED YOU ALREADY KNEW
WIFE 101 - EVERYTHING YOUR HUSBAND WISHED YOU ALREADY KNEW
THE MINISTER'S TOPICAL BIBLE
THE AFRICAN CULTURAL HERITAGE TOPICAL BIBLE
BISHOP C.H. MASON, Ithiel C. Clemmons
WITCHCRAFT IN THE PEWS, George Bloomer
THE BIBLICAL PRINCIPLES OF SUCCESS, Arthur Mackey
THE 1993 TRIAL ON THE CURSE OF HAM, Wayne Perryman
SINGLE LIFE, Earl Johnson
DAILY MOMENTS WITH GOD, Jacqueline E. McCullough
THE CALL OF GOD, Jefferson Edwards
THIS IS MY STORY, Candy Staton
LISTENING TO HER & UNDERSTANDING HIM, Sherman Watkins
PROPHETIC POWER, Kervin Smith
BODY BUILDING, Kervin Smith
ANOTHER LOOK AT SEX, Charles Phillips
WALKING THROUGH THE DOORWAYS OF DESTINY, Arthur Mackey
FIVE YEARS TO LIFE, Sam Huddleston

Pneuma Life Publishing
4451 Parliament Place
Lanham, MD 20706 U.S.A.
(301) 577-4052
(800) 727-3218
Internet: http://www.pneumalife.com